STAYING IN TOUCH WITH
GOD

STAYING IN TOUCH WITH
GOD

WENDELL JOYCE

Printed by Selah Publishing, Albany, OR. the views expressed or implied in this work do not necessarily reflect those of Selah Publishing.

ISBN 1-58930-022-X
Library of Congress Catalog Card Number: 2001088141

Dedication

To my nine-year-old son Andrew, who has been an inspiration to me. I am very proud of the strength and courage he has portrayed dealing with life and his walk with God. I pray that Andrew will always keep his faith and trust in God so that he will be an inspiration to others.

My Mom and Dad, who always instructed me of how important it is to have God in my life. I admire my parents for their strength and faith during the recovery of my Mom's cancer. I thank them for their support and standing with me while writing this book.

All my friends who have showed their support, encouragement, and prayers.

All those who read this book, I pray that these poems will bring encouragement and will be up–lifting to their soul.

Contents

Foreword 9

A Faithful Witness 11
A Heart That's Full Of Love 13
A Message In The Rain 15
A Savior Is Born 17
A Special Love For You 19
All Minds In One Accord 21
An Angel's Special Touch 23
Excuses 25
Faith In Miracles 27
Fears 29
Friends 31
God Will Be There For You 33
God Will Make A Way Somehow 35
God Will Send A Blessing 37
He's In The Midst 39
In God's Hand 41
Is Money The Answer To Change... 43
It Always Makes A Difference... 45
It's Not All Roses 47
Living By The Word Of God 49
Put On The Whole Armor Of God 51
Safe Inside The Storm 53
Seek After Righteousness 55
Survival 57

The Best Friend Of All 59

The Blood Is Still There 61

The Chosen 63

The Dividing Line 65

The Nine Fruits Of The Spirit 67

The Refreshing Rain 69

The Right Road To Travel 71

The Secret Garden 73

The Things You Do In Life 75

The Treasure Of A Man's Heart 77

Understanding The Will Of God 79

Using Your Talents For God 81

Walking With God 83

Who Or What Can Hinder 85

Your Reflection In The Mirror 87

Foreword

Life has many things to offer. But not every-
thing in life is what you hope that it will be. God
has given everyone the ability to make decisions for
the life they choose to live. But we don't always
make the best decisions. We find that pain, suffer-
ing and disappointment can be the result of not
making the best choices in life.

But by staying in touch with God, you can
always find the peace and the happiness that you
need in life. For when you take time to meditate by
praying and talking to God, it helps you to focus
and to have a better perspective of life. Even
though we are not able to see God with our eyes,
we can feel His presence deep inside our soul. And
just by talking to God alone, you can rest assure
that God hears and understands everything that
you need to talk to Him about. Because when you
need someone to talk to, you don't always feel that
everyone is really listening or understanding what
you feel inside. The best thing about talking to God
is that He knows you better than anyone and

understands exactly what you have been through. When someone has done you wrong, God knows all about it. For God doesn't have to guess or wonder about anything.

God is in control and has a plan to see you through when you put your faith in Him.

When you pour out your heart and soul to God, He always will give you the strength and the comfort that you need.

Because we all are human, we are prone to making mistakes. But by staying in touch with God who is perfect, we can enlighten our minds to make better choices in life.

–*Wendell Joyce*

A Faithful Witness

Lord I want to be your witness
no matter where I go;
and let my light shine
to everyone I know.

That I can stand for You
no matter what people say;
that they can tell I am a Christian
walking in the gospel way.

I know that I'm not perfect
trying to control this flesh within;
but please help me to be careful
to guard my soul from sin.

For I know that souls are watching
everything I say and do;
I hope that I can say something
to lead their soul to You.

I don't want to take part
in anything that is wrong;
or find myself somewhere
that I really don't belong.

There are so many things
that entice the eyes to see;

so remind me to stay focused
on what heaven has in store for me.

Let my soul have a testimony
from the reading of Your word;
that my voice can express it
somehow when my voice is heard.

To have the words of encouragement
to all of those around;
and to help one that's discouraged
that a smile can be found.

I would like to be more like You
and grow more in Your grace;
that the love of God will shine
and reflect upon my face.

I want to be a faithful witness
that is pleasing unto Thee;
that a soul would want salvation
by something they've seen in me.

A Heart That's Full Of Love

A heart that's full of love
is a heart that keeps on giving;
because there's something about that love
that makes their life worth living.

For they are always reaching out
to help someone in need;
especially caring for
a hungry soul to feed.

Not caring about the cost
or looking to be repaid;
because everything they need
from God it has been made.

Their life will not feel empty
but always will feel full;
because one that builds on love
has found a treasured jewel.

A jewel that helps in bad times
and even when one's sad;
for love is so refreshing
it can even make one glad.

Love has traits of patience
for it endures many things;

for it seems to have no boundaries
for the happiness that it brings.

Without love, life feels vacant
darkened and so cold;
without love, life has no meaning
for there is nothing left to hold.

For love gives strength and power
to those that help it grow;
for it even has an effect
on others that they know.

If one values their love to share
with a neighbor or a friend;
they'll find that love is a treasure
with rewards that never end.

For love is made complete
if the heart dwelleth in love;
and love is made perfect
by truly loving God above.

A Message In The Rain

One day my thoughts did wonder
why certain things take place;
to such good-hearted people
because of what they face.

And as I looked in the distance
hearing a sound from up high;
a crack as the sound of thunder
was moving across the sky.

A dark formation of clouds
started forming all around;
to bring great drops of rain
to pour down to the ground.

But as I kept on watching
I saw a lightning rod;
strike a tree that was part of
the great creation of God.

Its life was taken from it
for its beautiful sight to see;
its purpose in life is over
only leaving its debris.

Then a thought from the Bible
came into my mind;

which was a quotation of wisdom
that I stopped to search and find.

A quote "A time to plant
and a time to pluck up;
a time to break down
and a time to build up."

For God shows even in nature
things don't always turn out great;
by building back what was lost
there's a space of time to wait.

God waters all the flowers
the grass and the trees;
He nourishes them with sunlight
and gives them pollen from the bees.

God has made a purpose
for each and every thing;
to everything there is a season
for what life is going to bring.

A Savior Is Born

God worked out a plan
to provide a Savior for mankind;
so He looked for a perfect woman
on the Earth that he could find.

Highly favored was woman named Mary
that was chosen by God to bring;
forth a child to be called Jesus
to be a Savior, Lord and King.

It was proclaimed unto Mary
by one of the heavenly host;
that this child be born of a virgin
and conceived by the Holy Ghost.

This holy seed being immortal
would have a mortal life to live;
to offer the world salvation
is what Jesus Christ would give.

The birth of Jesus is recognized
by many of us today;
as a child that was born in Bethlehem
that we acknowledge on Christmas day.

This birth brought forth a tradition
of giving gifts to family and friends;

decorating trees with lights
joining together to sing Christmas hymns.

Not every Christmas decoration
shows what Christmas really means;
but what gives Christmas true meaning
are the nativity manger scenes.

Celebrating the birth of Jesus
can give one's spirit a joyful cheer;
but everyday can be just as special
just knowing His spirit is near.

What makes Christmas special
is taking the time to share;
some extra time with the Lord
giving honor to Him in prayer.

A Special Love For You

Christmas time is a special time
that comes just once a year;
as families join together
their hearts are filled with cheer.

As they adorn their trees with lights
and their gifts are wrapped with care;
manger scenes and angels
are displayed here and there.

To celebrate the birth
of Jesus our Lord and King;
as their voices join together
the carolers begin to sing.

Away in a Manger
and O Holy Night;
are songs that have great meaning
to lift their spirits bright.

They sing from their hearts sincerely
with their voices to give Him praise;
giving honor to Jesus of Nazareth
with love in their traditional ways.

For His love is not only felt
on this Christmas day;

but can be felt throughout the year
when one takes time to pray.

The special love of Jesus
can be felt upon every heart;
but for everyone to share this love
is left upon their part.

If you only think of Christmas
as just another Holiday;
then you're missing something special
that is so important about this day.

It's not the decorations
or the gifts that mean so much;
but it's giving praise to Jesus
that brings a special touch.

A touch that makes you feel
a love that flows straight through;
your body, soul, and spirit
because this love was made for you.

All Minds In One Accord

A church service runs much better
when all minds are in one accord;
because everyone can enjoy God's presence
when they worship to give praise to the Lord.

For how many really listen
when God's word is given to them;
or is a man only concerned
when something is said about him.

You find that people have too much
on their minds every day;
that when they go to church
their thoughts go a different way.

Someone may worry about a brother
or a sister that took their seat;
while another is constantly thinking
of what's waiting at home to eat.

While one man is sitting there wondering
when they'll pass the offering plate;
another man can't stop worrying
if the service is running too late.

Another man may feel burdened
that he's climbing more than a mountain;

while the man that's sitting right by him
enjoys drinking from God's fountain.

A sister may be busy looking
to see how everyone is dressed;
while a man in the congregation
may be leaning back to rest.

A certain one is thinking
about the bills that must be paid;
while another is busy wondering
about a car they want to trade.

A young boy may be busy
looking through different books;
and a young lady is constantly wondering
if the boys approve of her looks.

So often we sit in church
with wondering minds everywhere;
not thinking about the purpose
of what our minds are suppose to share.

For when minds are not cluttered
about tomorrow or yesterday;
one can focus on what God has to give them
instead of turning God's presence away.

An Angels's Special Touch

Messengers from God
are angels from up above;
created to watch over us
with a special kind of love.

Descending down from heaven
in a great mighty band;
are the angels sent from heaven
by God's almighty command.

For God is even among them
in His holy place;
where ever the angels are present
God reveals His grace.

Some angels may shine like lightning
having a raiment as white as snow;
while others appear in an earthly form
that you would not even know.

They may even seem invisible
or unseen by the human eye;
but when miracles are given
God's angels are standing by.

Angels which are very powerful
in strength and in might;

are guardians that are forceful
to protect us through the night.

For they have strong arms to lead us
and guide us as we walk through;
life's unexpected tragedies
and sadness that comes to you.

So if you ever wonder
how you made it through so much;
you may come to realize
it was from an angel's special touch.

Excuses

Putting God into your schedule
so often becomes delayed;
and when it's brought to your attention
an excuse is often made.

Giving time to God each day
sometimes all depends;
if one can spare some time
they spend with all their friends.

You may find that many Christians
are faithful to obligations;
but when it comes to going to church
they have no dedications.

Many will find the time
to run errands throughout the day;
but seldom do they find the time
to take out time to pray.

Some people have time for ball games
or frequent shopping at the mall;
but to find the time for God
they seem to have no time at all.

Some Christians very seldom
put the Bible in their hand;

because they use the excuse
"it's too hard to understand."

Some have busy careers
and are still eager to work overtime;
but how often are they eager
to give God some extra time.

God knows your daily schedule
and He knows what you need to do;
so finding the time for God
is really all left up to you.

With all the time that's wasted
what is God going to say?
when people tell God their excuses
on God's great judgment day.

Faith In Miracles

One may often wonder
if miracles are for real;
and if it's found in medicine
or some kind of pill.

It's not always easy
accepting illness that comes your way;
for at times you may feel that you
can't go through another day.

Some may get impatient
trying anything for a cure;
thinking they're feeling better
when they're really not for sure.

Doctors have helped many
with sickness by being concerned;
by using their great knowledge
and experience that they have learned.

Some have strong opinions
and beliefs in what they see;
but it's only by God's grace and mercy
of what is going to be.

A miracle may not happen
in a glorious or powerful way;

but just be thankful for all the prayers
that are answered when you pray.

We all may lack in faith
and believing in what might be;
because we keep looking
for what we want to see.

But God may have some other plan
than what you have thought;
and may have a certain time
for your miracle to be brought.

Don't ever give up hope
or believing that things will improve;
just keep praying and believing
that God is going to move.

When you least expect it
yours may be the case;
that you will see some kind of miracle
starting to take place.

Fears

There are things that we see
that cause our hearts to fear;
especially when it comes
to understanding things unclear.

For fear can be overwhelming
and can seem to control the mind;
stealing the search for courage
that the soul needs to find.

It can even be so cruel
to shake your soul inside;
and make you feel like running
to find a place to hide.

It can hinder you from doing things
that could be rewarding to you;
by making it seem impossible
to accomplish and make it through.

There may even be some people
that you're afraid to face;
for they make you feel uncomfortable
and even out of place.

It can make you feel defeated
thinking there's nothing you can do;

but feel that you'll make a mess of things
that will leave you sad and blue.

Your fears may seem wide as an ocean
making it harder for you to cross;
making you feel discouraged
and that your efforts have become a loss.

When you need strength and courage
and confidence inside;
just put your trust in God
to help push your fears aside.

Friends

God has made special people
that show such loving grace;
it seems to bring a smile
when you look upon their face.

They are the kind of people
that you always love to greet;
because of a special feeling
that takes place when you meet.

Sometimes their words are few
but just knowing that they're near;
is all that really matters
because they are so dear.

There seems to be no one
who can quite take their place;
because of that special love
that brings you to embrace.

There are those certain times
when you are apart;
that brings back special memories
that will always touch your heart.

Those times you've spent together
you cherish them so much;

it makes your heart feel good
and you want to stay in touch.

The relationship you share
with all your special friends;
is something that's so special
it has a love that never ends.

Although your time together
may at times seem so few;
but spending more quality time
sometimes is left up to you.

God Will Be There For You

I know your works
I know what you've done;
I see what you've been through
in this race that you've run.

I've seen all of the times
you felt you could not make it through;
but I want you to remember
that I'll be there for you.

Your way may seem rough
but try to keep up the pace;
try not to become discouraged
while running this race.

You may even stumble
by things in your way;
and worry about people
and what they may say.

For some people speak
from a cruel jealous heart;
trying to discourage you
from doing good on your part.

But who knows you better
than your heavenly Father above;

who has formed and created you
with His power and great love.

At times you've grown weak
and you may have thought that you failed;
but it was during all those times
your hands that I held.

I gave you the strength
so you could go another mile;
and I gave your heart laughter
when you could not seem to smile.

So you just keep going
with great courage to win;
and try to do your best
in this race that you're in.

I love you my child
always remember that I do;
so each day just remember
that I'll be there for you.

God Will Make A Way Somehow

Sometimes your luck can change
and things can turn out bad;
and steal your moment of laughter
making your heart feel sad.

You might even feel defeated
with some anger, pain or fear;
when you see how it can affect
the ones that you love so dear.

For your loved ones are so special
and they mean so much to you;
sometimes you don't want them to worry
about what you are going through.

A loved one can bring you strength
when you feel like you could cry;
by showing their kind affection
and knowing that they're close by.

But if you still are having a battle
with what you are going through;
sometimes just getting through it
is all left up to you.

Sometimes things just happen
for what reason you may not know;

but if you allow your thoughts to linger
you will just keep feeling low.

But if you pray to God sincerely
and to Him you humbly bow;
and believe that God will move for you
God will make a way somehow.

God Will Send A Blessing

You may not always understand
why certain ones are blessed;
for many can do such evil deeds
and act as though they've lived the best.

But not every man that's blessed
will have a life that's blessed to keep;
"For whatsoever a man soweth
That shall he also reap."

For God knows every person
and he knows what each man needs;
and God grants different blessings
according to each man's deeds.

If your always thankful for how God's blessed you
then you'll always have a blessing to share;
and your blessings will mean more to you
than for someone that just don't care.

How does one describe someone
being blessed in many ways?
It could be how one trusts in God
or maybe how one prays.

Some people don't have a lot in life
but are blessed better than what man can see;

because their life with God means more to them
than all the treasures of the sea.

For some people don't need a lot
to feel satisfied inside;
because God is really all they need
for their blessings to abide.

Count your blessings daily
and be thankful for everyone;
and give God some special thanks
for all your troubles that have gone.

If you're waiting for God to bless you
more than He has before;
just give Him praise every time you can
because your praises He don't ignore.

God has many blessings
that He will give to you;
especially when you give Him praise
in everything you do.

God will truly bless you
if you humbly come to Him;
for all those who sincerely love the Lord
God will send a blessing unto them.

He's In The Midst

This battle that I'm in
that I seem to keep on facing;
brings back reminding thoughts
that my mind keeps on placing.

At times I begin to wonder
if I've really done my best;
to try and make it through
this trial and this test.

When it seems too rough
and too hard for me to bear;
I try to remind myself
that life's not always fair.

For at times there has been sadness
that filled my eyes with tears;
how long will the pain last
is what my heart fears.

But I know that there is hope
when I kneel down and pray;
for God gives me strength and courage
so I can face another day.

When God's spirit comes down upon me
and I feel Him deep inside;

it gives me reassurance
that He will be my guide.

And if this battle continues
then I must always persist;
and keep praying to my Lord and Savior
for I know He's in the midst.

In God's Hand

The problems that you face
may seem to be tough;
and even make you think
that you sure had enough.

It's hard to endure problems
that last for very long;
because you start to wonder why
and what you've done wrong.

The feeling of worry
may start to press upon your mind;
by thinking of solutions
and the answers to find.

If you worry about problems
it might make you lose sleep;
and even build up emotions
that may cause you to weep.

But God knows every situation,
every problem and every sin;
He even knows of your weakness
and every place that you have been.

God knows each time you pray
and each decision that you make;

He knows just what you're going through
and how much you can take.

So when you've done all that you can
the Bible says to stand;
because the answer that you're waiting for
is waiting in God's hand.

Is Money The Answer To Change The Way You Live?

If you had enough money
to change the way you live;
what things would you keep
and what things would you give?

Without any limitations
to hinder your desire;
would your expectations be the same
or would they be much higher?

Would your heart be compassionate
to a soul you see in need;
or would you tend to have
a heart of selfish greed?

Could you live where you do
or would you move far away;
or would the memories that you have
encourage you to stay?

Would you keep all your possessions
or would you want everything new;
Would you be thinking of your family
or just be thinking about you?

Would you become a different person
or would you try to stay the same;

would you try to use your money
to bring you fortune and fame?

Would you be more contented
than you were before;
or would it only make you
want more and more?

Would it bring you happiness
or would it bring you sorrow;
wondering what you will do
with all your money tomorrow?

Would you give to charity
or a church that you know;
or put your money in the bank
and just watch your money grow?

If you live for God
would your devotion still be there;
or would your heart have a change
to where you just don't care?

Money can surely buy you
a lot of different things;
but you're not always satisfied
with the happiness it brings.

If a man will only realize
what's best for the life he leads;
is to trust God fully
to supply all his needs.

It Always Makes A Difference When Jesus Passes By

There are times in our lives
when the way grows dim;
and seeking for comfort
of peace seems slim.

The hours in thought
with the pain that you feel;
searching for an answer
while waiting to heal.

Can you really hold up
in this time of despair?
is the question you ask
when trying to prepare.

Will the tears stop flowing
from the feelings inside;
or will it burst like the waves
that bring in the tide.

The heart gets so heavy
trying not to complain;
for it needs some relief
that will ease up the pain.

Though friends try showing
that they really care;

but that don't release the pain
in your mind that's still there.

But with thoughts and prayers
and on faith you lean;
that's when you'll find Jesus
has come on the scene.

For prayer is the answer
that makes things change;
no matter how small
or big they may range.

Your way will seem brighter
and you'll understand why;
for it always makes a difference
when Jesus passes by.

It's Not All Roses

Sometimes when you look at life
it can seem to be so unfair;
for there seems to be so many burdens
that we all have to bear.

The birth of a child is a miracle
and many are born every day;
but so many are not loved
and their parents just give them away.

It seems that when we grow up
and we take a look at our past;
we have some fading memories
and see that time has went so fast.

We so often rush to work
trying our best not to be late;
and sometimes it's an appointment
that is scheduled on a certain date.

Many parents take their children
to school and they pray;
"God watch over our children
and keep them safe in your arms today."

Many have went to lay down
or to rest in their easy chair;

when suddenly a call awakes them
with unpleasant news to share.

Sometimes we wait for the doctor
with our hearts filled with despair;
hoping that the doctor
will give the best kind of care.

So often we lose a loved one
and we grieve upon their grave;
thinking of all the great memories
and the friendship that they gave.

"It's not all roses"
is a thought of wisdom to say;
when things just don't turn out
in the right kind of way.

But with God we have hope
if we trust Him and obey;
by praying and believing
in God's word every day.

Living By The Word Of God

When you read the word of God
and apply it to your life;
you will find a better way
to deal with sin and strife.

When you read the scriptures
and study what you have read;
your soul will feel contented
because your soul is being fed.

The word of God is pure
enlightening to the eyes;
and if read with great desire
it can even make one wise.

The amazing thing about God's word
is when you read each page and turn;
it has a way that when it's read
each day there's more to learn.

It shows that no one's perfect
but encourages you to do your best;
especially when life may seem
more than a trial and a test.

Words to give encouragement
and words to reassure;

words to give you discipline
to change you from what you were.

It speaks of being sharper
than any two-edged sword;
for it pierces the soul and spirit
where the thoughts of the heart are stored.

When problems seem to arise
stop and take time to read;
and search the word of God
to find help for your need.

Living by the word of God
with the whole heart applied;
will give you more love and joy
with your soul being satisfied.

Put On The Whole Armor Of God

We must be strong in the Lord
to have the power of God's might;
to stand against the powers of darkness
that arise with a raging fight.

We must stand against the wiles of the devil
but we are never told to attack;
because it is God who fights our battles
and moves the enemy off our back.

When we walk through paths of unrighteousness
we must always be ready to stand;
having on the Whole Armor of God
with the Shield of Faith held in our hand.

When those fiery darts of the wicked
are thrown to pierce our soul;
we will hold up the mighty Shield of Faith
to show that God is in control.

We must have the Breastplate of Righteousness
by living a righteous and holy life;
having the truth girded within us
to help ward off sin and strife.

With our feet shod with the Gospel of Peace
we can stand anchored to hold our ground;

for we can stand being immovable
by the peace from God that's found.

We will take the Helmet of Salvation
that gives us confidence to see;
that when we submit to God
the devil has to flee.

When we hold the Sword of the Spirit
and we understand what it can do;
we find what a powerful weapon
God has given to help us through.

We must Pray without ceasing
to give us strength to carry on;
and watch with Perseverance
with Supplication for everyone.

For by praying one for another
we become stronger every day;
for God will supply our needs
when we take out time to pray.

For one day our battle will be over
and God will lead us out;
to our home in heaven
that the Bible talks about.

Safe Inside The Storm

Storms sometimes are violent
raging with a mighty force;
and can cause a lot of damage
when it sets in to take its course.

Sometimes they come unexpected
leaving little time to prepare;
but you may still have time
to call out to God in prayer.

For God allows the storms to come
but we must let Him see;
that we know God has the power
in His hands to set us free.

Even though the storms may rage
there's really no need to fear;
because God is in control
and the storm is His to steer.

God can make us feel secure
by His presence we feel inside;
knowing that God is in control
and in Him we can confide.

Just as fast as the storms may come
can the storms be moved away;

for God can speak "peace be still"
and even the winds and seas obey.

God is a safe haven of shelter
as His arms reach out to form;
a strong shield of protection
that is safe inside the storm.

Seek After Righteousness

To find a life of happiness
might seem hard to find;
depending on the source
and what is on their mind.

To seek for earthly treasures
and luxuries galore;
might leave the heart uncontented
and always wanting more.

If your world becomes surrounded
by things for only you;
you might find that your friends
lose interest in what you do.

If your heart is full of envy
of another man's gain;
you might decide to do something
that will only cause you pain.

In thoughts of a dream
that one hopes to come true;
depends on their effort
and what they try to do.

With so many choices
that you have to make;

the decisions that you decide on
affect each step you take.

But if you lose focus
and you don't know what to do;
remember there is a Savior
that will reach His hand to you.

If you seek after righteousness
you'll find that God will make you whole;
giving you a life of happiness
and contentment within your soul.

Survival

Survival is very important
in order for one to live;
but there's always something to sacrifice
and time that you must give.

Life's not always easy
and may at times seem unkind;
but if you look in the right direction
the essential things you'll find.

Often you search for an answer
when deciding which step to take;
sometimes you learn the hard way
by accepting you made a mistake.

Experience is your best teacher
if you learn with an open mind;
if you watch very carefully
a guideline you will find.

Endurement may seem rough at times
but needful to make it through;
by strengthening your abilities
that lie inside of you.

When people who love causing trouble
seem to get in your way;

it's best to be very cautious
and weigh out the words you say.

When a message is brought to you
of sad news or someone's death;
you try to ease your mind with peace
by taking a deep breath.

For those who have children
worry will always be there;
but one can always find peace of mind
if they turn to God in prayer.

The Best Friend Of All

A friend shows their love
by showing that they care;
and it shows by their concern
with the time that they share.

Willing to accept you
for just being you;
not trying to change you
or the things that you do.

Always ready to forgive you
even when you make a mistake;
because your friendship is something
that they don't want to forsake.

Happy to rejoice
for all the things that you receive;
and by being very supportive
in all the things that you believe.

They are there to give you encouragement
when life seems to get you down;
trying their best to bring you laughter
somehow to erase your frown.

Trying to bring you peace
when anger stirs inside;

giving you words of wisdom
to help your anger to subside.

There is really one true friend
that you can always find close by;
who will listen to all your problems
and give you comfort when you cry.

When you think of all your friends
and which one you should call;
your friend whose name is Jesus
is the best friend of all.

The Blood Is Still There

God did not make us perfect
allowing the flesh to live within;
showing it takes a spiritual life
to help protect the soul from sin.

For sin is not something
that just happens overnight;
but develops when you continue
doing things that are not right.

And once sin has taken place
and has planted its seed;
the mind has no way of knowing
of where it's going to lead.

So if you find that you have sinned
or journeyed the wrong way;
don't wait too long to ask the Lord
for forgiveness when you pray.

For our sins are forgiven
in faith believing by His grace;
for Jesus will wash away every sin
that has taken place.

For all have sinned and come short
of the glory of God's plan;

by allowing the flesh to desire things;
that look good in the eyes of man.

Even though Jesus died
for our sins many years ago;
everyone can receive forgiveness
for the Bible tells us so.

The Bible explains it clearly
so everyone can share;
so we can have reassurance
that the blood is still there.

The Chosen

Chosen are the hearers
and doers of God's word;
on their knees in faith believing
that their prayers have been heard.

For God sees them when they're praying
when things have turned out wrong;
He turns their sorrow to gladness
and they start rejoicing with a song.

They try not to argue
or quarrel to get their way;
trying to be so careful
of everything they say.

Working to be peacemakers
when anger builds up strife;
trying to sort out feelings
they don't need in their life.

When tempted to do something
they know that is not right;
they know it's just not worth it
because they want to be a light.

Their daily time in prayer
and reading the Bible in their hand;

is what they find is needful
to make it easier to stand.

When idle talk or rumors
are whispered in the ear;
the chosen will try to find some way
so they don't have to hear.

The chosen may seem different
or peculiar in one's eyes;
but God has chosen foolish things
that will confound the wise.

The Dividing Line

There is a dividing line
that a Christian should never cross;
in order to protect his soul
and salvation from suffering loss.

For once you take a step
and you try to cross the line;
your conscience will start to warn you
by giving you a sign.

It will give you an eerie feeling
to make you stop and think;
that what you just have done
is what caused your heart to sink.

Because what you start to feel
is a change taking place;
by making you feel different
by God's amazing grace.

And each time you say a word
that you know you shouldn't say;
you will immediately catch yourself
without any delay.

If you find yourself
somewhere you shouldn't be;

a feeling starts to warn you
advising you to flee.

And when your among people
who say just anything;
your heart will feel a cringe
by the comments that they bring.

But if you should decide
to cross over the dividing line;
you will feel out of place
and your light will no longer shine.

The people that are around you
will take notice right away;
that your light is no longer shining
like it did every day.

So remember it's important
to live the best you can;
to allow God's loving grace
to shine from you to man.

The Nine Fruits Of The Spirit

There are nine fruits of the spirit
that every Christian heart can bear;
and when they begin to produce them
they have something great to share.

Love which is compassionate
and can always be found;
with forgiveness from the heart
to give everyone around.

Joy that is outstanding
for the excitement it will show;
their great desire to serve God
reveals their happy glow.

Peace that will push heartache
and pain far away;
by focusing on God
with prayer throughout the day.

Long-suffering that endures
many hurtful things;
with endurance to bear itself
through what life so often brings.

Meekness that is so humble
with a special kind of grace;

that shows upon their smile
when you look upon their face.

Gentleness that is so careful
not to speak an unkind word;
weighing out each word that's said
before their voice is heard.

Goodness that shows kindness
to everyone they meet;
with a nature that's so pleasing
just by the simple way they greet.

Faith that is devoted
in what God is going to do;
because they trust and believe
that God's promises are true.

Temperance that will always
display self-control;
in every situation
they learn obedience for their soul.

If a Christian decides to keep these fruits
they must produce them everyday;
so that sin doesn't try to come
and pick their fruits away.

If you produce some of these
you're really doing good;
but if you produce all of these
you're living like you should.

The Refreshing Rain

The earth became so dry
with no moisture to retain;
because it struggled for many weeks
without a drop of rain.

But as people joined together
praying that God would hear their plead;
God blessed the earth with rain
to show He blessed their need.

For now everything in sight
appears so fresh and clean;
for the grass that once was brown
has returned to its color green.

The plants that once were limp
have now sprung forth to show;
how the soft suddle rain
was essential to help them grow.

And as the soft suddle rain
gently touched my face;
it brought a refreshing feeling
that I could not displace.

For my soul was so refreshed
by what I saw in view;

the earth in its natural beauty
looked the way that I once knew.

After knowing what God has blessed
to replenish what I see;
it gives me faith to believe
He can answer prayers for me.

For God has ways to comfort you
when certain things make you cry;
and release the realm of pain
that makes your soul so dry.

By seeing how that prayer
can change many things;
you know when prayers are answered
what a blessing that it brings.

If God can refresh the earth
with rain to help it heal;
then God can refresh a soul
with His spirit that you can feel.

So if you need God to refresh you
with something you're going through;
just ask God to allow
His spirit to rain down on you.

The Right Road To Travel

The road of life can be hard to travel
when you don't know which way to go;
especially when it seems so different
from what you used to know.

It can seem as though things have changed
from what they used to be;
and finding the right road to travel
is not visible for you to see.

For if man does not keep watching
the road he travels there in;
he will stop paying attention
and forget where he has been.

Sometimes a man might detour
thinking he has found a better way;
but after traveling a great distance
he has strayed too far away.

And after traveling the wrong road
so far that he loses track;
it's not always that easy
for him to find his way back.

But when a man loses track
and cannot focus in his mind;

he should stop and ask God to direct him
to the right road he needs to find.

There always is a reason
a man travels the wrong road;
it's usually when he is distracted
or from carrying a heavy load.

To follow another traveler
may not be the best thing to do;
for his road may not be
the road that's right for you.

For God knows every road in life
that every man has took;
and the right road is always there
that man will overlook.

The best advice for a man
is to take out time to pray;
and ask God for His guidance
as he travels through the day.

The Secret Garden

There is a secret garden
where I can go each day;
it's a place to find escape
when I just need to get away.

A place where I can go
when I need to meditate;
when I need to sort out problems
that I need to evaluate.

It's not a garden of flowers
with butterflies in flight;
but it has peace in the valley
that gives my heart delight.

Neither does it have the essence
of fragrant flowers to smell;
but it works like aroma therapy
that keeps my senses feeling well.

For when I'm not feeling well
it gives me comfort to caress my soul;
for here I can find the healing
that I need to make me whole.

Whether the sun outside is shining
or if the clouds are filled with rain;

there's always a refreshing feeling
I know that's there to gain.

It takes away my burdens
that sometimes get me down;
and some how I feel such happiness
that turns my life around.

And when I'm feeling lonely
and just need someone to care;
here I know I can feel a presence
that I know is always there.

It's a place where I find a refuge
when I'm running from a storm;
for I find it has a shelter
with a strong and mighty form.

It is here that I find serenity
I know that's always there;
for what this secret garden is
it's a place I find for prayer.

For in prayer I talk to God
for He knows what's best for me;
and the more I talk to God
the better person I can be.

The Things You Do In Life

The things you do in life
will create the person that you are;
and as long as you succeed in life
it will challenge you to go far.

You can learn a lot by watching
other people doing things;
but just be careful what you duplicate
to your life for what it brings.

If you try to be someone
other than yourself;
then all your doing is leaving
the real you on a shelf.

When you see you've made mistakes
take it as a lesson that you've learned;
because if you learn from your mistakes
there is great wisdom you have earned.

Try not to become discouraged
when things don't turn out right;
just stand and have the courage
to face them with all your might.

If no one seems to believe
that you will succeed in what you do;

just having faith in yourself
is the best encouragement for you.

Going through life's most tragic moments
can help one to realize;
that there is hope for tomorrow
if trouble should arise.

When trying to make hard decisions
just keep this thought in mind;
could something good become of it
or is trouble the result to find.

If something seems to hinder you
from doing the best you can;
God can change every circumstance
because He always has a plan.

God will never leave you or forsake you
as long as you fully trust in Him;
and for everyone that obeys His word
He will send a blessing unto them.

If you want a life of happiness
then let God be your guide;
because you will always succeed in life
when God is on your side.

The Treasure Of A Man's Heart

The treasure of a man's heart
holds what a man so much adores;
what he cherishes most in life
are the treasures that he stores.

It would be every man's delight and pleasure
to enter a place beyond compare;
where there's nothing but peace and contentment
and wondrous beauty everywhere.

The Bible describes a place
beyond the heavens we see above;
that is prepared for everyone
that is perfected in God's love.

And by this it's through repentance
where such perfection can be done;
when a man can see his faults
and ask forgiveness from God's son.

For through the blood of Jesus Christ
a special cleansing will take place;
that washes and makes one clean
all because of His amazing grace.

This cleansing is to purify
to make a man holy within;

to sanctify all the uncleanness
that brought forth the sin.

But it is left up to man
to keep all uncleanness out;
and to live a holy life
that the Bible talks about.

"Be ye holy for I am holy"
is what God speaks in His word;
to walk in the light and not in darkness
is the message that man has heard.

And even though Christian beliefs
are not all the same;
a man must not have spot or wrinkle
but should be holy and without blame.

It is a holy way
that God wants man to live;
and in return God has the greatest
treasure in heaven to give.

If the treasure of a man's heart
was to live holy every day;
what he would treasure most in life
would be to please God in every way.

Understanding The Will Of God

Understanding the will of God
is not always easy to receive;
but comes by praying and seeing
what God has allowed you to achieve.

Asking God for His guidance
for the answer you need to find;
will help give you the direction
of what God has in mind.

When your purpose in life becomes
unclear for you to see;
just keep praying for understanding
of what God wants you to be.

For everyone's purpose
in life is not the same;
and sometimes you may wonder
if life is just a game.

You may even question
when things are not right;
but just keep trusting and believing
God with all of your might.

When God becomes most important
and it's clear for you to see;

that God being the overseer
of your life is the key.

Then life will have new meaning
in things that you face;
giving you a better perspective
of what will take place.

For soon a light of hope
will begin to shine through;
giving you the answer
that God has in store for you.

Using Your Talents For God

Special talents lie
within each and every heart;
but to reveal those special talents
will rely upon your part.

Talents may come so natural
to a lot of people that you see;
but don't allow their special talents
to discourage what yours can be.

You may have certain fears
or a lack of confidence inside;
that may interfere your showing
the talents that you hide.

Sometimes it take overcoming
the fears in your mind;
to reach those expectations
that you hope to find.

Every man and woman
may have a certain limitation;
but to achieve the feel of confidence
it takes work and dedication.

If you've ever tried to do something
and feel you've made a mess;

don't give up but keep on trying
until you've made success.

You may feel that your efforts
have been a struggle and a fight;
but great talents do not usually
develop overnight.

God has a special talent
that He will give to you;
when you work with the talents that you have
doing the best that you can do.

Working for God can inspire
other people that you know;
and encourage them to work for God
by the talents that you show.

If you use your special talents
by working for the Lord;
God will bless you for your efforts
with a blessing He has stored.

Walking With God

If there seems to be something missing
with the way that you live;
then try a walk with God
and see what He can give.

A walk with God is special
because of His spirit you feel inside;
the happiness He gives to you
is something you can't hide.

God will be your best friend
one like you've never had before;
and the more you desire His friendship
your heart will cherish Him more.

God is always there to listen
even when your words seem few;
and God is always available
when you need someone to talk to.

A walk with God is better
than any exercise you do;
for His strength and endurance
will build up inside of you.

The more time you spend with God
the better person you will be;

for a change will take place
that even you will see.

As long as you keep walking
with God every day;
your burdens will seem lighter
than they did yesterday.

The more you walk with God
a greater blessing you have in store;
for God has great benefits
that are worth waiting for.

If a closer walk with God
becomes your main goal;
you'll find the greatest treasure
to give to your soul.

Who Or What Can Hinder

There are many devoted Christians
who live for God each day;
by reading the word of God
and taking out time to pray.

At church they worship God
to strengthen their soul inside;
and learn what the Bible teaches
to cast their cares aside.

But who or what can hinder
a man of God today;
except for the man of sin
that works to hinder his way.

Satan knows that a man battles
with the flesh against the spirit;
so he uses lustful things
to entice the flesh to it.

For the lust of the flesh entices
causing curiosity to build;
making sin look so desirable
that the flesh will want to yield.

But once the flesh starts yielding
it will not be satisfied;

until it gives into temptation
that has been building up inside.

When the flesh has finally tasted
the desired pleasure of sin;
the thrill will in time diminish
from the boundaries that it's in.

Every time the flesh is fed
by what sin has to give;
the flesh starts taking space
where God's spirit use to live.

For sin is what hinders
the spiritual part of man;
and keeps a man of God
from living the best he can.

Although a man's not perfect
but can sin and make mistakes;
a man can be forgiven
for every sin that he makes.

If he asks God to forgive him
as he humbly bows to pray;
the blood of Jesus redeems him
and his sins are washed away.

Your Reflection In The Mirror

When you look into a mirror
a reflection is what you see;
which is a part of God's creation
that He created you to be.

You may not always approve
of the image that's in view;
but accepting how God made you
is all left up to you.

And over time there are changes
that you will see taking place;
when you look into the mirror
to look upon your face.

Some people are so beautiful
with looks so sharp and bold;
but beauty is only skin deep
that one day will grow old.

But as you look upon the surface
of your flesh that's made of clay;
you can see how God has made everyone
in a different kind of way.

But you must look much deeper
than what this reflection has to show;

a part inside your body
that God gave you to control.

Your mind to make decisions
through what life has to give;
and you can make the choice
for the way you want to live.

But there is something deep inside you
that lies within your heart;
it's your soul that makes the image
the most important part.

God gave you a soul for a reason
so that you could decide;
if you would allow your creator
to come and dwell inside.

For when you allow God's spirit
to dwell inside your soul;
your body feels an inner peace
that makes the body feel clean and whole.

For when God's spirit dwells inside you
there is an image that portrays;
the reflection of God
through you throughout the day.

For this flesh that you look upon
will someday decay;
but your soul can live forever
when God calls your soul away.

To order additional copies of

STAYING IN TOUCH WITH
GOD

have your credit card ready and call

(800) 917-BOOK

or

send $9.99 plus $3.95 shipping and handling to

Selah Publishing
P.O. Box 708
Albany, OR 97321